Christmas Activities

for KS2 Language and Literacy

Irene Yates

Other books in the series
Christmas Activities for KS1 Language and Literacy   ISBN 978 1 903853 66 5

Christmas Activities for KS1 Maths   ISBN 978 1 903853 68 9

Christmas Activities for KS2 Maths   ISBN 978 1 903853 69 6

Published by Brilliant Publications

Sales and despatch:
 BEBC Brilliant Publications
 Albion Close, Parkstone, Poole, Dorset, BH12 3LL
 Tel: 01202 712910
 Fax: 0845 1309300
 email: brilliant@bebc.co.uk
 website:www.brilliantpublications.co.uk

Editorial and marketing:
 Unit 10, Sparrow Hall Farm, Edlesborough, Dunstable
 Bedfordshire LU6 2ES

The name Brilliant Publications and its logo are registered trademarks.

Written by Irene Yates
Illustrated by Gaynor Berry
Cover design by Z2 Repro
Cover illustration by Chantal Kees

ISBN 978 1 903853 67 2

First published in 2004, reprinted 2008.
10 9 8 7 6 5 4 3 2

Printed in the United Kingdom
© Irene Yates 2004

Contents

Year 5 (continued)

Introduction

This book has been designed to take you through the term leading up to Christmas, with the targets of the Key Stage 2 Literacy Strategy autumn term for Years 3–6 specifically in mind. The book, as a whole, covers a wide spectrum of these targets whilst providing lots of fun activities all linked to Christmas.

The sheets can be used independently and most ask the child to work in the space provided. There are just a few activities which require extra sheets of paper. Each task, or activity, has educational rigour, making the work suitable for introducing a topic or reinforcing it. The sheets are not designed as time fillers and should not be used as such. They are meant to become an integral part of the teacher's literacy planning for the first term of the year.

The comments in the reindeers' speech bubbles usually reflect upon the concept being tackled. They give ideas for the focus of plenary discussion sessions. For example, page 9 uses homonyms and gives the teacher a chance to talk about 'practice' and 'practise'; page 10 offers an opportunity for discussion about verbs, nouns and missing subjects, such as the 'I' missing from 'I thank you.'

Some of the sheets ask the children to share their reading and their writing with other members of the group and this should be encouraged wherever possible.

The contents page shows the exact literacy target for each page, and gives a brief description of the objective of that target. The book is divided into four sections, one for each year, and provides targets for Word, Sentence and Text levels in the order in which they occur in the Literacy document. Using the brief description for each objective you can run down the contents page to find objectives that you may wish to reinforce with any particular children. You can tick off the level references to remind yourself of targets you have worked on.

Have fun!

Christmas presents

Underneath the Christmas tree are lots of presents. In the presents there are:

a b**oa**t

a tr**ai**n

a f**or**t

a b**ear**

a k**i**t**e**

a b**ow**l

monster t**ee**th

a b**ir**d

a c**ar**

Write down all the words you know with the same sounds in the middle or the same spelling pattern.

ai	ea	i_e	ee	oa	ow	ar	ir	or
train	bear	kite	teeth	boat	bowl	car	bird	fort

How many words did you get?

Which sound do you know most words for?

Snowman wordsearch

Find these words in the snowman. The words can go forwards, backwards, up, down and diagonally.

about
after
again
back
brother
came
could
down
from
good
half
help
home
jump
little
make
many
next
once
over
push
should
some
them
very
water
what
with
your

```
          b  a  c  k  x
          t  b  d  p  r  f  s
          v  e  r  y  w  r  x
          q  u  z  o  l  o  m
          m  a  k  e  t  m  f
       h  w  a  t  e  r  h  s  e
       w  h  l  i  t  t  l  e  m
    r  h  a  l  f  p  r  s  c  r  a
    d  r  c  a  b  o  u  t  h  r  f
 o  o  d  t  g  p  u  s  h  g  c  t  h
 v  w  r  h  a  s  t  h  o  m  e  e  p
 e  n  h  e  i  t  r  o  s  t  p  r  m
 r  n  d  m  n  x  d  d  r  y  s  r  u
 c  e  d  o  t  e  h  l  o  y  o  y  j
 h  e  l  p  n  s  u  n  w  m  n
 s  y  n  a  m  r  o  n  c  e  c
 h  l  d  e  m  a  c  w  h  a  t
 g  s  h  o  u  l  d  h  l
 w  i  t  h  y  o  u  r  i
```

Make a wordsearch of your own, using these words:

have
here
one
school
two
when
who

Ask your friend to do it.

Christmas words

Read the Christmas words in Column 1 carefully, one by one.
Practise saying the letters out loud.

Copy each word in column 2.

Cover up the word in column 1 and 2 and write it from memory in column 3.

Check your spelling.

Column 1 Read	Column 2 Copy	Column 3 Try
Christmas		
year		
presents		
star		
stable		
baby		
angel		
celebrate		
cards		
merry		

How many new spellings have you learned?

I keep getting them wrong.

Just try again. I'll help you.

My Christmas words log

Write all the words you know about Christmas in your word log. The pictures will help you.

Christmas words I know	Spelling practice	
	Word	**How I can remember it**

Practise your spellings till you get them right.

I AM practising.

Thank you letters

Draw circles round all the verbs.

Dear Gran
I thank you for the skateboard.
I am sorry about the flowers in
the garden but you can grow
some more.
Love
Tom

Dear Aunty Jo
I really liked the jumper
you knitted me. I liked it
so much I made a blanket
for the dog's bed with it.
Love from
Gemma
x x x

Dear Uncle Ant
Thanks for the fishing
rod. When can we go?
I am ready when you are.
Love from
Josh

Dear Grandad
Thanks for the Christmas sweets
you made. I was only sick five
times.
See you soon,
Love from
Katy

Dear Mum and Dad
Thank you for the trampoline you
bought me for Christmas. It will
save me using my bed.
I love you.
Isabel

Dear Jack
Thanks for the live tarantula.
My mum screamed when she
saw him. Unfortunately we
don't know where he's gone.
Love from
Sam
P.S. Can you get me another
one?

Talk about how the
same word can be a
noun or a verb.

Hint
Think about 'thanks' and 'thank you'. One is a
noun and one is the verb. How can you tell
which is which?

What about 'love from' and 'I love you'?

Christmas conversations

Write these bubbles out as speech with speech marks.

Let's go see!

I think Santa's been.

_____ said Henry.

_____ Jamie shouted.

Shhh ...
be quiet.

I'm trying to
be quiet.

_____ said Henry.

_____ answered Jamie.

Wow!
Lots of presents!

How many are
for me?

_____ said Henry.

_____ asked Jamie.

Let's sort
them.

_____ suggested Henry.

Any for me?

_____ Dad shouted down the stairs.

Any for me?

Reindeer

Each reindeer is carrying a bag of punctuation marks. Can you name them?

Do you know?

1. When to use full stops?

_____

2. When to use capital letters?

_____

3. When to use question marks?

_____

4. When to use exclamation marks?

_____

5. When to use commas?

_____

6. When to use speech marks?

_____

Write three sentences using all of the marks.

Get a friend to check them.

Santa's News Weekly

Pretend you are the editor of **Santa's News Weekly**. Write an article for the front page. Don't forget to use headlines and sub-headings.

Did you see what happened last night?

No, I was asleep.

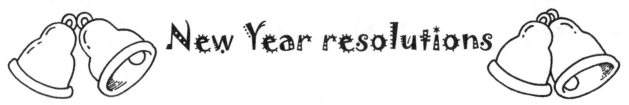

New Year resolutions

Read Sam's New Year resolutions. They don't really make sense because he has forgotten to write them in sentences. Mark where you think the sentences begin and end. Write them out again with full stops and capital letters. Lay them out in a neat list.

These are my new year resolutions I will never borrow my brother's play station without telling him I will always clean my teeth before I go to school if mum tells me to go to bed I won't argue I will do my homework every night every day I will be early for school I will feed the hamsters and give them water french fries and burgers are out I will eat loads of cabbage I will never say yuk

Sam

Cabbage?

Yuk.

Santa's workshop

Read the story.

It was the week before Christmas. Santa's workshop was so busy that no one had time to think. Everybody rushed around, backwards and forwards, treading on each other's feet. There were so many toys in the loading bay that there was hardly room for any more. The parcels stretched from floor to ceiling and from wall to wall.

More parcels kept being trundled in on the loader. There were big parcels, little parcels, cubes, spheres, bike-shaped parcels, long, fat parcels, short, flat parcels – in all the colours of the rainbow. The noise of the parcels being loaded and unloaded was deafening. Suddenly Santa shouted out, "Everybody stop!"

The loading bay went silent. Nobody moved. What could be wrong?

"Somebody," said Santa in a very cross voice, "has forgotten to put the labels on!"

Where does the story take place?

Which part of the story describes the setting?

Which words and phrases describe the setting?

Draw a picture of the workshop, using the description to help you.

Write what you think happened next.

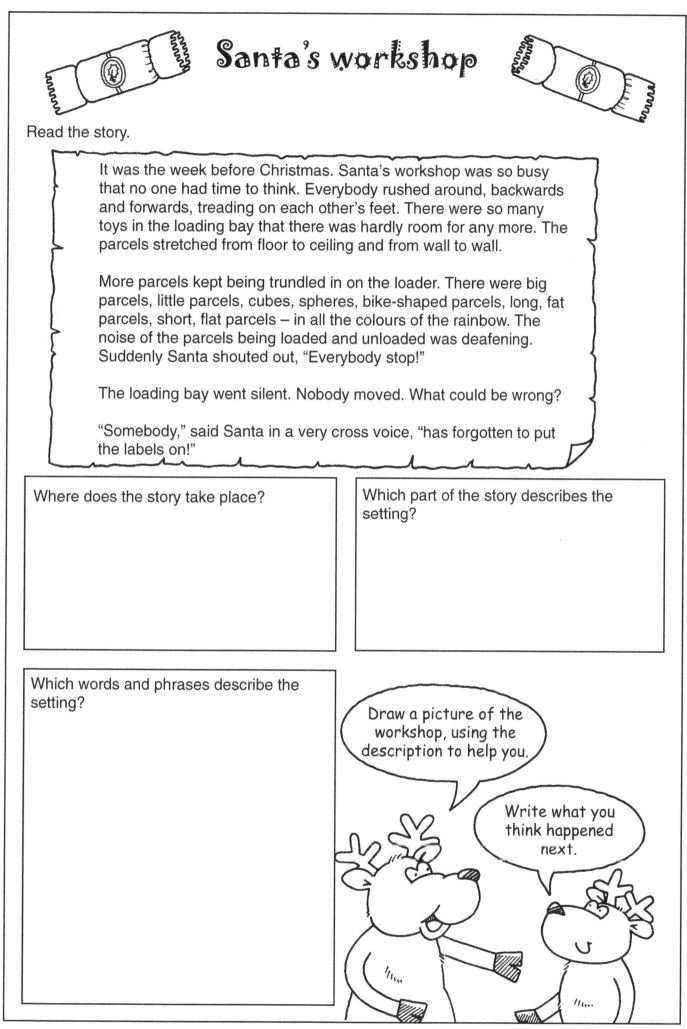

Christmas places

Think of four different places where Christmas stories might take place.
Write the story opening for each place, describing your setting.

Christmas poems

Make up some shape poems. Write a list of Christmas words first, to help you.

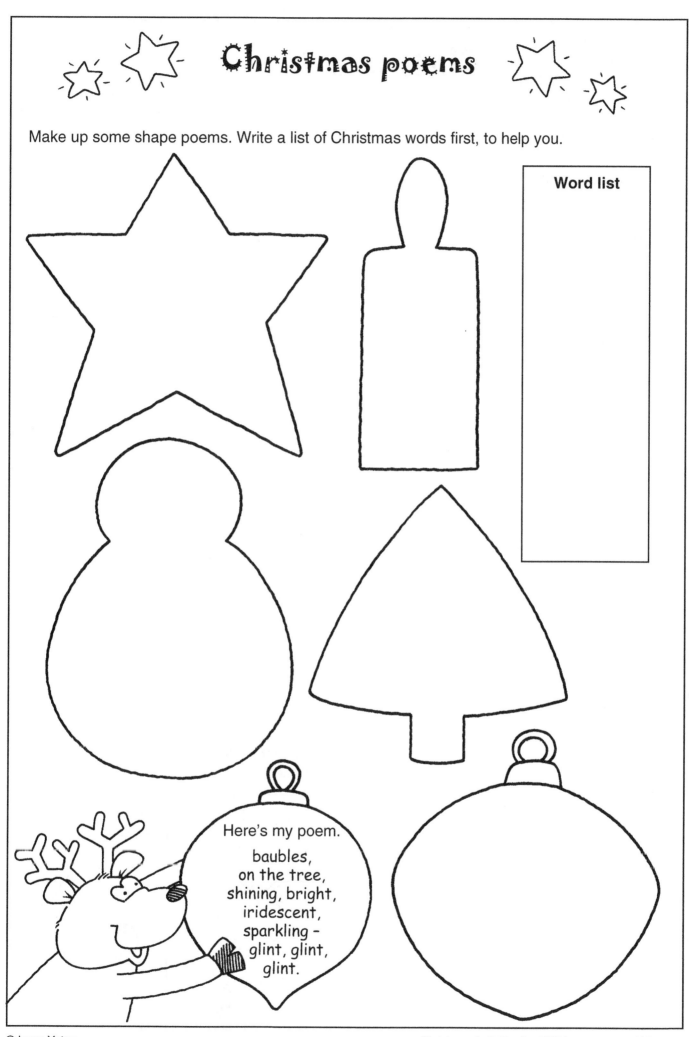

Word list

Here's my poem.

baubles,
on the tree,
shining, bright,
iridescent,
sparkling –
glint, glint,
glint.

 # Christmas drama

You need to be in pairs or threes. You are going to write a Christmas play.

Talk together about:
* theme (Is it a nativity? Or not?)
* characters
* what happens

Use another sheet if you need more room.

Read your plays aloud and compare them.

Bethlehem

Remembering everything you know, write a report about the birth of Jesus.

Title	
When did it happen?	
Where did it happen?	
What happened?	
Who was there?	
What were the gifts?	

I remember it.

Don't be silly. There were NO reindeer!

Christmas tree wordsearch

Find these words in the Christmas tree. The words can go forwards, backwards, up, down and diagonally.

another
been
boy
brother
by
called
did
door
first
girl
have
here
house
how
just
love
more
much
old
our
people
right
rough
sister
that
these
tree
two
were
when

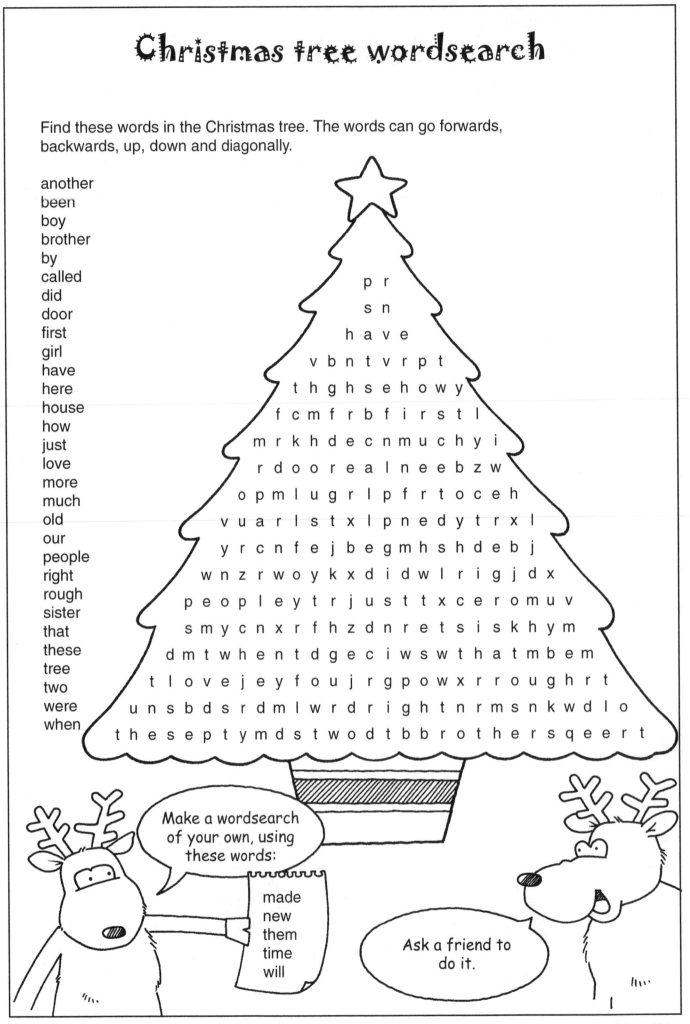

Make a wordsearch of your own, using these words:

made
new
them
time
will

Ask a friend to do it.

Christmas food

These are all things that have been traditionally eaten at the Christmas feast.

How many syllables does each word have? Write them on the correct plate.

turkey
plum pudding
stollen
fruit
nuts
roast potatoes

marzipan
Christmas cake
trifle
sausage rolls
shortbread

mince pies
chocolate log
ham
goose
oranges

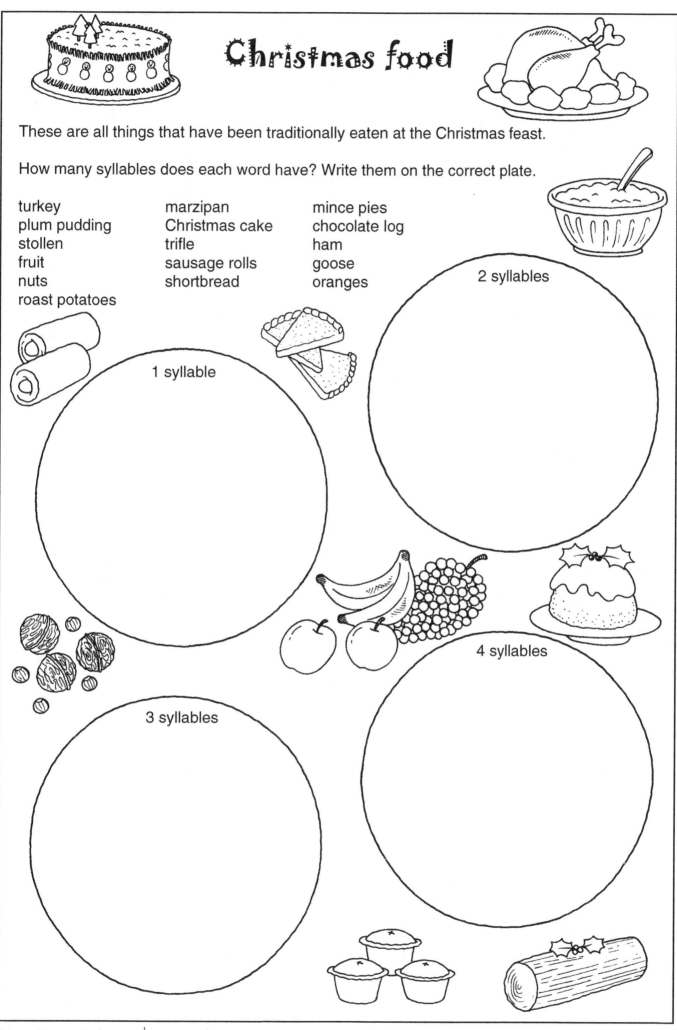

1 syllable

2 syllables

3 syllables

4 syllables

Yuletide meanings

Fill in the yule word-log.

Word	I think it means	My dictionary says	Another dictionary says
yule			
celebration			
advent			
nativity			
custom			
feast			
festival			

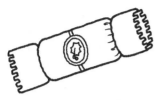 # Christmas fun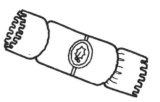

Make a collection of words that describe Christmas. Give each word your own definition, then look it up in a dictionary and write the dictionary definition. Two words are shown, to help you.

Word	My meaning	Dictionary meaning
1. fun	having a good time	amusement, e.g. at a fair
2. merry	happy time	joyful, full of laughter
3.		
4.		
5.		
6.		
7.		
8.		

What's your best word to describe Christmas?

Exhausting!

 # Christmas storyboard

Here is a storyboard, written in the present tense. Write the story but make sure all the verbs are in the past tense.

Storyboard

* make a list
* buy the presents
* buy the cards
* wrap the presents
* write the cards
* put up the decorations

* fetch the tree
* decorate the tree
* go to church
* welcome the visitors
* have a wonderful day
* say/write thank you

I'm eating my Christmas hay.

No! You ate your Christmas hay.

Testing, testing

Santa's a bit mixed up. He has things to do and things to carry. But he doesn't know which is which. Test whether these words are verbs or nouns by deciding if the tense can be changed. Spot the words which are verbs **and** nouns!

Word	Can the tense be changed?			What kind of word is it?
	Past	Present	Future	
give				
snow				
reindeer				
deliver				
chimney				
climb				
carry				
hurry				
glide				
drop				
world				
travel				

Use the words to write a story.

Which tense?

Christmas power

Read this unfinished poem.

In the midnight sky, a star _____

And angels _____

Above the hillside, shepherds _____

And _____

Across the world, three kings _____

with gifts.

At an inn, a family _____

to be safe.

In a stable, a mother _____

Into a manger, a baby _____

to sleep.

Around the crib, animals _____

Then everyone _____

The first Christmas _____

And all over the world _____

Make a list of all the different verbs and phrases you can think of to add to each line.
Choose the ones you think are the most powerful to complete the poem.

Decide on a title for your poem.

Read your poem aloud to the class.

Snowball synonyms

A thesaurus is a kind of dictionary. It gives you alternative words that mean almost the same as the word you are looking up.

Use a thesaurus to find synonyms for each word in a snowball. Add as many snowballs as you can to each pile. One has been started for you.

nice

beautiful

excellent

lovely said give got cold wanted bright

An 'antonym' is a word that means the opposite.

Can you add an antonym snowball on top of each pile?

Christmas lists

Write some Christmas wish-lists. Remember to put in commas between each item on the list, but not before or after the 'and' at the end. Make your lists as much fun as you can.

Mum wants

Dad wants

The dog wants

My best friend wants

My teacher wants

I want

Your wish items do not have to be 'things'.

For instance, Mum might want some peace and quiet!

Write a Christmas story

This page will help you to plan your story. Just make notes.

Plan
Title:
Author:
Who is the main character?
Who are the other important characters?
What will you main character do?
How will the characters treat each other?
How will the characters cope with what happens?
How will the story end?

Now write your story.

Share it with a friend.

What's Santa's background?

Write a biography of Santa's life. Make it as interesting as you can.
What do you think might happen to him in the future?

Letter from Santa

This letter is to **you** from Santa. Fill in your name and read the letter carefully.

Dear _____

Everything has gone wrong this year because I slid over in the snow and broke my arm. I can't drive the sleigh. Could you come and do Christmas for me? I would be very grateful.

Love Santa

P.S. Let me know how you would organize Christmas Eve night.

Write your reply to Santa:

Well, that looks like being fun!

I hope _____ doesn't forget our carrots!

Christmas Eve

Write a poem about the magic night of Christmas Eve. There are words and phrases in the stars to help you. You can use them, or they might help you to think of some good words and phrases of your own.

high above the rooftops

frost

starlit

distant

snowflakes drift

silver moon

silence of the night

shadows

glittering

light of candles

dead of winter

glistening

star in the east

midnight hour

Make a Christmas card and write your poem in it.

Make a Christmas card

Look at the pictures carefully, then write the instructions out very clearly. Make sure they are in the right order. Use bullet points.

You need:

This is what you do:

✳

✳

✳

✳

✳

✳

✳

1.

2.

3.

4.

5.

6.

Ask a friend to follow your instructions.

Do the instructions work?

Santa's spellcheck challenge

Santa challenges you to read these anagrams and, using spelling strategies, work out what the words are. They are all words you should know well.

4 letters
aawy
abby
abck
abot
aglo

5 letters
abcel
aadls
aamez
ackns
acgim

6 letters
aegmnr
aegnor
aaglxy
aalswy
amoott

7 letters
aabbceg
aabceln
aacegkp
aaceknp
aaddgnr

8 letters
aabdekry
aabdhlln
aabehlpt
aaccertu
aacgiimn

9 letters
acgillnor
achimrsst
achinirst
aclmoorss
adeerstyy

Can you work out what this Christmas word is?

aceefiknnrs

Make up an anagram puzzle for your friend to solve.

Santa's grid game

You need two players for this game. Each player needs one sheet. Both players use the first grid on their own page. When you have filled in all the spaces in that grid, play the next grid, and so on.

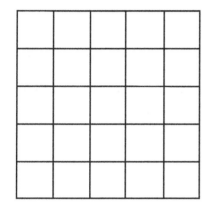

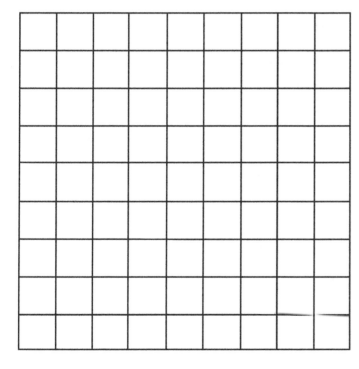

What you do.
Take turns to call out any letter of the alphabet. Each player writes the letter in any space on their own grid, trying to build up words that read across or down, or both.

Score points for each word you make. The winner is the player who has the most real words.

Santa's panto puzzle

Santa loves a pantomime. He also loves puzzles.

This puzzle is all about words ending with vowels other than the letter 'e'.
Read the clues to find the words.

1. A marsupial

2. A huge spider

3. A type of dog

4. A musical instrument

5. A Japanese poem

6. An Inuit lives in one

7. You take pictures with it

8. A Spanish dish

9. Type of Italian food

10. A mountain that erupts

11. It's red but is it a fruit or a vegetable?

12. You need it when it rains

13. A kind of antelope

14. A yellow fruit

15. To travel over snow

16. Sound reflection

When you know the
words, write their
plurals.

Santa says 'best foot forward'

Santa uses a lots of idioms. When he says:

Best foot forward.

he means

Get going with as much speed, effort and determination as possible.

Sometimes his helpers can't understand him. Draw lines to match the phrases to their definitions.

1. There are too many problems to see the whole situation.

Wait till they're in the land of nod.

I can't see the wood for the trees.

4. It's impossible to find.

2. This is unlikely to happen.

I've got my eye on you.

It's a needle in a haystack.

5. Wait till they're asleep.

3. I'm watching you.

Pigs might fly!

Get your skates on!

6. Hurry up.

Write the meanings beside your idioms.

Think of some idioms of your own.

Victorian Christmas

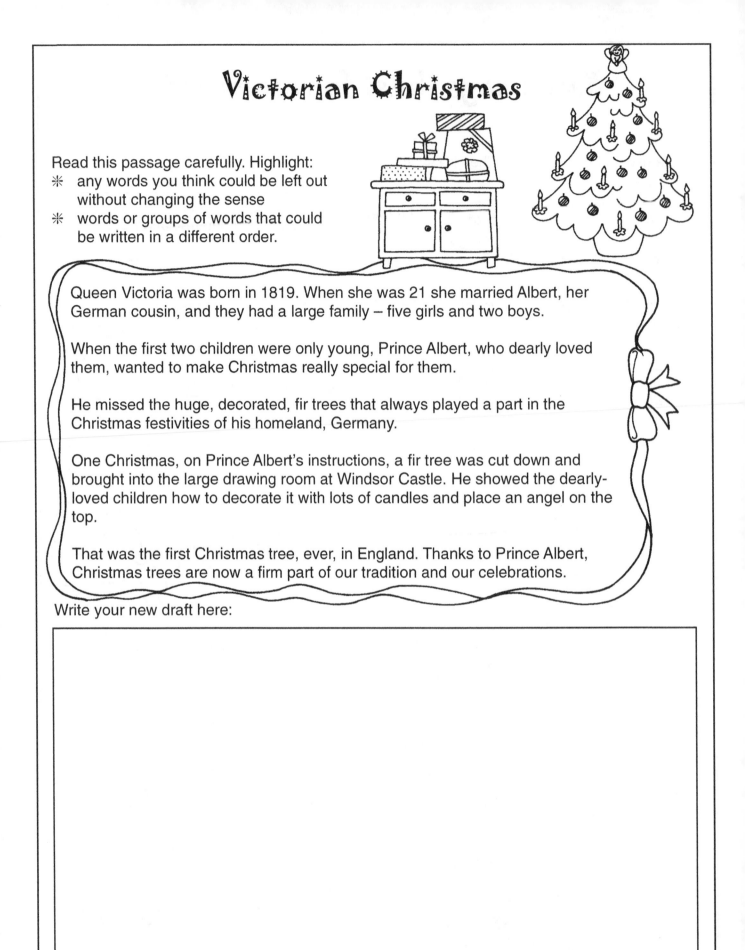

Read this passage carefully. Highlight:
* any words you think could be left out without changing the sense
* words or groups of words that could be written in a different order.

Queen Victoria was born in 1819. When she was 21 she married Albert, her German cousin, and they had a large family – five girls and two boys.

When the first two children were only young, Prince Albert, who dearly loved them, wanted to make Christmas really special for them.

He missed the huge, decorated, fir trees that always played a part in the Christmas festivities of his homeland, Germany.

One Christmas, on Prince Albert's instructions, a fir tree was cut down and brought into the large drawing room at Windsor Castle. He showed the dearly-loved children how to decorate it with lots of candles and place an angel on the top.

That was the first Christmas tree, ever, in England. Thanks to Prince Albert, Christmas trees are now a firm part of our tradition and our celebrations.

Write your new draft here:

Twelfth Night

Read this information passage carefully:

Twelfth Night is January 6th. It is also known as Epiphany. It is when the three wise men came from the East to Bethlehem, to greet the baby Jesus.

The word for the three wise men is Magi. The Magi were famous for their wisdom. They had learned everything they could and were able to read the future from the position of the stars in the sky.

The Magi's names were Melchior, Caspar and Balthazar. They brought rich gifts to show that Jesus would become really important. The gifts were gold for a King, frankincense for a high priest and myrrh for a great healer.

Write the passage again, in your own words, for a much younger child to read. You could turn it into a story if you wanted to.

Family Christmas

Read the following script, then turn it into a piece of narrative. Take special care of how you set it out, using speech marks and spacing. Try to use a selection of different speech verbs and describe how the characters speak.

Charlie: What do you want for Christmas, Nan?

Nan: I don't know. Anything.

Charlie: Chocolates?

Nan: No, not chocolates. Too fattening.

Charlie: A new pair of slippers?

Nan: No, Charlie. Not slippers. My old ones are comfy.

Charlie: Something soapy?

Nana: No I've got lots of soapy things.

Charlie: What then?

Nan: I don't know, Charlie. Anything.

Hint:
Here are some speech verbs: said, whispered, asked, shouted.

Write your narrative here:

One starry night

Recap the story of the birth of Jesus, so that you know all the facts. Put yourself into the place of one of the people involved.

Write your own story about what happened, from that person's point of view. Take great care with the verbs.

One starry night, I ...

Christmas party 1

Read this passage. It is from Chapter 2 of *A Christmas Carol*, by Charles Dickens.

In came a fiddler with a music-book, and went up to the lofty desk, and made an orchestra of it, and tuned like fifty stomach aches. In came Mrs Fezziwig, one vast, substantial smile. In came the three Miss Fezziwigs, beaming and loveable. In came the six young followers whose hearts they broke. In came all the young men and women employed in the business. In came the housemaid, with her cousin, the baker. In came the cook, with her brother's particular friend, the milkman. In came the boy from over the way... In they all came, one after the other; some shyly, some boldy, some gracefully, some awkwardly, some pushing, some pulling; in they all came, any how and every how.

Fill in the chart:

Character	Words which tell you what the character is like	What you can tell about the character from what the words tell you

Take your favourite character and write a description of him or her from what you think you know. Say why you think you know this.

Christmas party 2

When you have read and discussed the passage on 'Christmas party 1', imagine that you are going to have a great Christmas party yourself.

You can invite anybody you like. Write your own introduction here, in the style of Charles Dickens.

In came...

You can write what happened at the party on another piece of paper, if you want to.

Christmas party 3

Read the passage on 'Christmas party 1' again.

Answer these questions:

Pictures in your mind
What pictures do you see in your imagination?

Are you part of the picture or are you standing on the outside, observing?

Interacting with the text
What feelings does the text give you?

Which words, phrases or sentences really hooked you when you were reading?

Predicting
What do you think happened next?

How do you think the party scene will end?

Write an atmospheric poem

Write a poem that evokes a strong atmosphere of the writer being alone at Christmas. Try to convey the feelings and moods of the writer by choosing your words and phrases very carefully.

The words and phrases in the holly leaves will help you, but don't just use them as they are. Try to use them to help you think of your own ideas.

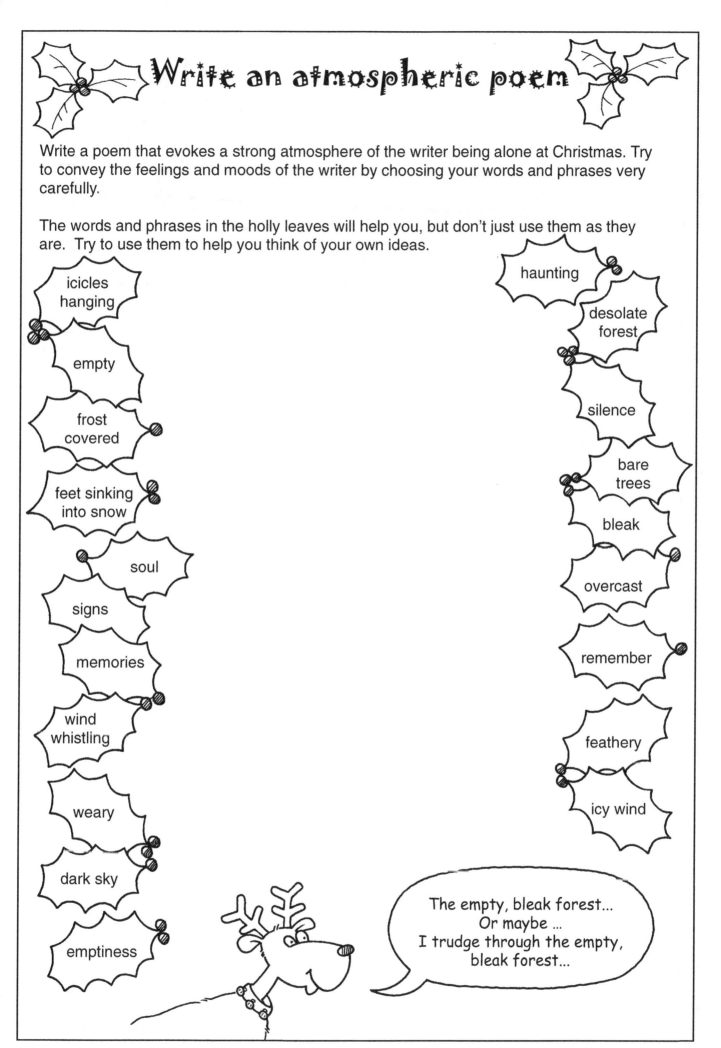

icicles hanging

empty

frost covered

feet sinking into snow

soul

signs

memories

wind whistling

weary

dark sky

emptiness

haunting

desolate forest

silence

bare trees

bleak

overcast

remember

feathery

icy wind

The empty, bleak forest...
Or maybe ...
I trudge through the empty, bleak forest...

The best Christmas I ever had

Think about all the Christmases you have had. Which one sticks in your memory the most for good reasons? Imagine you are entering a competition to write about your very best Christmas. The competition judge is not known to you. You really want to win the prize.

Write your recount:

How to make a pop-up Father Christmas

Look at the pictures. They show you how to make a pop-up Father Christmas. Write the instructions so that someone can make one.

What you need:

What you do:

1.

2.

3.

4.   5.

6.

I'm making a pop-up reindeer instead.

Try your instructions out on a friend.

How to make a Christmas decoration

My chosen decoration is

You will need

Diagram or drawing

Use this box to draw a diagram of what you are explaining.

This is what to do:

Explain each stage in this box, for example:
1. First, ...
2. Then you ...
3. Next you ...
4. Finally, ...

Christmas is a good thing

I think Christmas is a really good thing because …

The reasons I think this are, first, …

Secondly, …

Another reason is …

So …

Summing up, my idea is …

Could you write a piece to say why Christmas is not a good thing?

Easy. I have to work too hard!

Christmas cracker words you need to know

Read the clues to fill in the crackers.

1. A book about your own life

   a

2. A short well-known saying

   p

3. A section of writing, beginning on a new line

   p

4. A group of letters at the beginning of a word

   p

5. A book containing synonyms

   t

6. A phrase that compares one thing with something else

   s

7. A book about someone else's life

   b

8. A group of letters at the end of a word

   s

9. Words like 'as', 'in', 'between', 'on'

   p

10. A way to help you remember a tricky spelling

    m

11. Words

    v

12. The study of words and their origins

    e

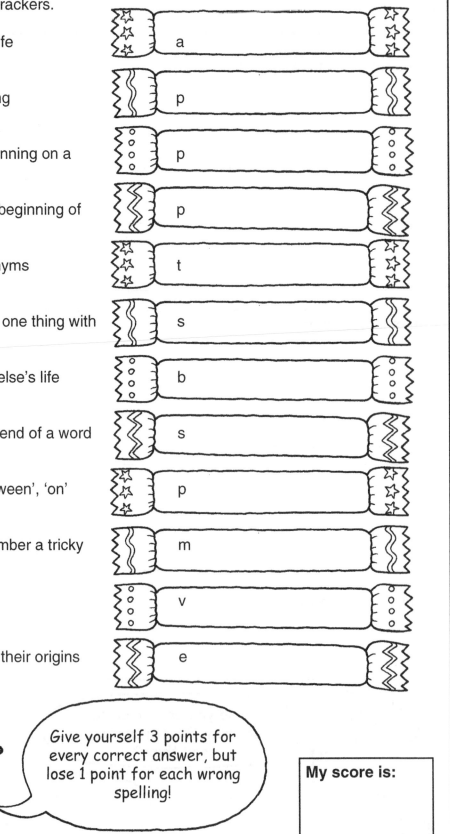

Give yourself 3 points for every correct answer, but lose 1 point for each wrong spelling!

My score is:

Christmas spelling journal

New words I have come across this term	Words to practise	
~~Bethel~~ Bethlehem	Bethlehem	🌲🌲🌲

Give yourself 3 Christmas trees for every word you have learned. How many Christmas trees have you got?

Use the dictionary to check.

Christmas glossary

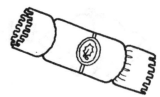

New words I have learned	Meaning/definition

Make sure your spelling is correct. Use a dictionary or the spellchecker on the computer.

Presents under the tree

Have a look at the letter strings on the labels. Decide for each one whether it is a prefix or a suffix. Write one word in each present for each letter string.

aero

audi

aqua

duo

cede

graph

micro

ex

hydro

photo

hydra

in

prim

scribe

bi

cred

con

scope

oct

port

tele

tri

clude

sub

Use a dictionary to help you.

Check your spellings with the dictionary or the spellchecker.

Christmas past

The following words are all ones you might read in old Christmas carols or old Christmas stories. Write what you think they mean.

Old word	Meaning
beauteous	
betrothed	
hasten	
hath	
hither	
methinks	
methought	
thither	
thou	
thy	
whither	
yea	
yonder	
yore	

Methinks I'll get me a bag of oats.

Yoicks!

Celebrations

Have a look at the sentences below. Some are **active** and some are **passive**. Transform each group of sentences into the other, by swapping the subject around. Write your new sentences underneath.

For example:
Active: Father Christmas left loads of presents.
Passive: Loads of presents were left by Father Christmas.

> **Hint:**
> A verb is active when the subject in the sentence performs the action.

Active sentences

1. The whole family joined in decorating the Christmas tree.

    _____

2. Dad cooked turkey with all the trimmings for dinner.

    _____

3. Grandma pulled a cracker with Dad's help.

    _____

Passive sentences

1. Presents were opened by everyone.

    _____

2. In the afternoon, a party was greatly enjoyed by all the family and neighbours.

    _____

3. The whole street was lit up by a million lights.

    _____

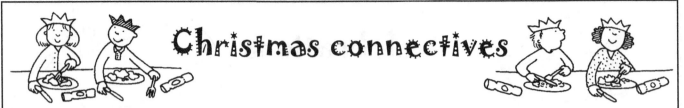

Christmas connectives

Have a look at the following sentences. Then look at the connecting words (connectives) in the box. Use the connectives to add bits to make interesting sentences out of the boring ones. Turn the sentences into a Christmas story. Add as many connecting bits as you need.

Boring sentences
1. Christmas dinner was cooked.
2. The presents were unwrapped.
3. Grandad fell asleep.
4. Billy ate too much.
5. The boys fell out.
6. All the lights went off.
7. Everybody laughed.
8. There was a loud bang.
9. Nobody did it.
10. A fight broke out.

Interesting sentences!

Connectives			
while	beside	nearby	under
first	far away	when	if
second	then	by	unless
next	as long as	only	like
just	as	before	because

Christmas clever

How clever can you get at forming complex sentences?
A simple sentence is:

> Mum wrapped the presents.

You can add clauses and connecting words to make a much more complex sentence.

> Choosing the best possible wrapping for each one, Mum wrapped the presents even though she knew they would all, in their excitement, tear off the paper without even looking at it.

Use this complex sentence as a model to write your own in place of these:

The sled sped down the slope.

The snow melted.

Dad switched on the lights.

Gran said, "Thank you."

Joe cleared away.

The robin pecked.

The party ended.

"Happy New Year," someone shouted.

An unbelievable Christmas

Read the following true story. Write it below with proper punctuation.

Christmas eve 1914 it was bitterly cold two armed forces faced each other across a strip of foreign land the british and the germans there was a clear night sky the guns were silent the silence was hung with fear the germans were sad thinking of home they set up a christmas tree in their trench a symbol of home suddenly the british soldiers heard singing from the german trenches silent night holy night they began to join in soon all the soldiers were singing a german soldier crossed the line then another and another a british soldier joined them they began to shake hands across the barbed wire that separated them happy christmas happy christmas they all shouted.

Hint
You will need to use:
* 27 capital letters
* 14 full stops
* 4 commas
* 2 colons
* 2 semi colons
* 2 sets of quotation marks
* 2 exclamation marks
* 4 paragraphs in total

Mr Pickwick on the ice

Mr Pickwick, created by Charles Dickens, is one of the most famous characters in English novels. In this extract, Mr Pickwick and his friends are sliding on ice.

This is the voice and style of Charles Dickens.

> The sport was at its height, the sliding was at the quickest, the laughter was at the loudest, when a sharp, smart crack was heard. There was a quick rush towards the bank, a wild scream from the ladies, and a shout from Mr Tupman. A large mass of ice disappeared; the water bubbled up over it; Mr Pickwick's hat, gloves and handkerchief were floating on the surface; and this is all of Mr Pickwick that anybody could see.

Read the passage two or three times to get the feel of how Dickens writes. Then, pretending that you are Charles Dickens, write the paragraph that might come next.

Everyone knows Cinderella...

So there's this girl who has a wicked family. She goes to a disco and meets a prince...

Write the story of Cinderella in your very own words. Try to stick to the framework of the story but make it modern – happening now.

Plan the story first, using the 'Cinderella – spot the difference' sheet.

Can we have reindeer instead of white horses?

Who wants reindeer when they can have a stretch limo?

Cinderella - spot the difference

	Original version	Modern version
All about the heroine		
All about the hero		
Other characters		
What happens at home		
What happens next		
How it ends		

Nativity play

Write the beginning of the nativity story as a play.

Remember to include:
* List of characters
* Setting
* Stage directions
* Well thought out dialogue

Try out your script with friends.

Write the rest of the play.

S. Claus: curriculum vitae

Write a curriculum vitae (CV) for Santa Claus. Make sure you include all relevant information. Make it fun.

Find out the true story of Saint Nicholas...

and write a CV for him! Compare your two CVs.

Answers

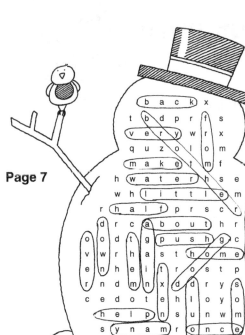

Page 7

Page 34

4 letters
away
baby
back
boat
goal

5 letters
cable
salad
amaze
snack
magic

6 letters
manger
orange
galaxy
always
tomato

7 letters
cabbage
balance
package
pancake
grandad

8 letters
daybreak
handball
alphabet
accurate
magician

9 letters
carolling
Christmas
Christian
classroom
yesterday

Reindeer's word
frankincense

Page 36
kangaroo
tarantula
corgi
piano
haiku
igloo
camera
paella
spaghetti
volcano
tomato
umbrella
gnu
banana
ski
echo

Page 37
I can't see the wood for
the trees – 1
It's a needle in a haystack
– 4
Get your skates on – 6
Wait till they're in the land
of nod – 5
I've got my eye on you – 3
Pigs might fly! – 2

Page 50
1. autobiography
2. proverb
3. paragraph
4. prefix
5. thesaurus
6. simile
7. biography
8. suffix
9. prepositions
10. mnemonic
11. vocabulary
12. etymology

Page 54
beautiful
engaged
hurry
have
here
I think
I thought
there
you
your
where
yes
over there
a long time ago

Page 55
Passive
1. The Christmas tree
was decorated by the
whole family.
2. Turkey with all the
trimmings was cooked by
Dad for dinner.
3. A cracker was pulled
by Grandma, with Dad's
help.

Active
1. Everyone opened
presents.
2. In the afternoon, all the
family and neighbours
greatly enjoyed a party.
3. A million lights lit up
the whole street.

Page 58
Christmas Eve, 1914. It
was bitterly cold. Two
armed forces faced each
other across a strip of
foreign land: the British
and the Germans. There
was a clear night sky; the
guns were silent. The
silence was hung with
fear.

The Germans were sad,
thinking of home. They
set up a Christmas tree in
their trench: a symbol of
home. Suddenly the
British soldiers heard
singing from the German
trenches. 'Silent night,
Holy night.'

They began to join in;
soon all the soldiers were
singing.

A German soldier crossed
the line, then another and
another. A British soldier
joined them. They began
to shake hands across the
barbed wire that
separated them. 'Happy
Christmas! Happy
Christmas!' they all
shouted.

Page 20

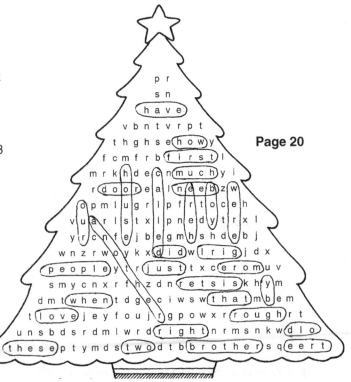